This book is designed to be a
your own discovery of the ci
Inside you will find 100 facts
marvellous and magnificent,
ridiculous! I leave it up to you to traverse the
city of Worcester and find the locations,
statues, shops and more mentioned here and
return with even more knowledge!

If you have a fact of your own, use the pages in
the back to write it down, and always let me
know too!

I travel around the UK visiting cities and towns
collecting interesting facts to tell the world in
my books. If you are interested in facts about
another city or town, I most likely have a book
about it!

If you want to contact me please do! I'd be
happy to take on suggestions for future
projects. Or just tell me an interesting fact
about your home town. Send me an email at
LizzieWintersBooks@gmail.com.

Thanks, and enjoy!          *Lizzie Winters*

# 1

Worcester is the capital of the county of Worcestershire, based in the West Midlands.

1.

Other notable towns in the county are Evesham, Kidderminster, Redditch, Bromsgrove and Great Malvern.

Worcester is by far the largest location in the county, and in fact the only city in the county.

# 2

The River Severn runs right through the centre of Worcester.

Britains longest river starts in the Welsh mountains and runs through Shropshire, Worcester and ends up in the flatlands of the Severn estuary.

The river runs right next to the grand Worcester Cathedral and is a beauty spot for tourists and locals alike.

# 3

In 1084 the first bricks were lain for what was to become the modern Worcester Cathedral, but the cathedrals roots actually began 400 years earlier, in the year 680.

# 4

Worcester is by far the largest town or city in Worcestershire, and is growing fast.

The most recent census in 2021 revealed the population to be 103,872.

The population hit just over 102k in 2017 but steadily declined up until 2020. There was then a sharp rise of over 3000 people, hitting the total of almost 104,000.

# 5

Worcester was heavily damaged by a fire in 1202, which destroyed much of the city centre.

The fire began in a tannery and quickly spread, destroying over 300 homes and killing many residents.

# 6

The famous composer Edward Elgar was born in the village of Broadheath, near Worcester, in 1857.

Elgar is known for his patriotic and sentimental works, including the famous "Pomp and Circumstance" marches.

# 7

Elgar's music has been performed at the Three Choirs Festival, which is held in Worcester, Hereford and Gloucester every three years since 1715.

The festival celebrates choral music and has become an important cultural event in the region.

# 8

The Worcester porcelain factory, which was established in 1751, became one of the most famous manufacturers of fine china in the world.

The factory produced exquisite porcelain pieces that were sought after by wealthy collectors and royalty.

# 9

Worcester was an important centre for the wool trade during the Middle Ages, and became a centre for cloth-making in the 16th century.

The city's location on the River Severn made it a convenient hub for transporting goods, which contributed to its economic growth.

# 10

The name Worcester is derived from the Old English words "Weorgoran ceaster", meaning "Roman fort by the River Severn".

The name evolved over time, eventually becoming the Worcester we know today.

# 11

Out of 354 English Districts, Worcester takes the 237th spot.

Birmingham hits top spot with 1,001,200 population and Isles of Scilly props the table up with just 2,100.

Worcester is down as 94,300 in 2015.

# 12

Worcester was founded by the Romans in the 1st century AD as a military settlement.

The Roman fort was established to control the crossing of the River Severn and to act as a base for military campaigns in the surrounding area.

# 13

The city was also badly damaged during the English Civil War, when it was besieged by Parliamentary forces.

The Royalists held Worcester for several weeks before finally surrendering to the Parliamentarians, resulting in significant damage to the city.

# 14

The Battle of Worcester, which took place in 1651, was the final battle of the Civil War, and resulted in a decisive victory for the Parliamentarians.

The battle was fought on the outskirts of the city and was one of the bloodiest battles of the war.

# 15

The city has a range of shopping options, from independent boutiques and gift shops to larger chain stores.

The Crowngate Shopping Centre is the city's main shopping destination, with a wide range of high street brands and restaurants.

# 16

The Worcestershire County Cricket Club is based at New Road in Worcester and has a rich history of success, including several County Championship titles.

# 17

Worcester is home to a number of historic churches, including St. Andrew's Church, which dates back to the 11th century, and St. Swithun's Church, which is famous for its unique architecture and beautiful stained glass windows.

# 18

The Worcester Warriors are a professional rugby union team based in the city.

The team plays at Sixways Stadium and has a strong following among local fans.

# 19

The Commandery is a historic building in Worcester that was originally built as a medieval hospital. It later served as the Royalist headquarters during the Civil War, and is now a museum that explores the city's history.

# 20

Worcester has a thriving arts and culture scene, with a range of events and festivals taking place throughout the year. These include the Worcester Festival, which features music, theatre and comedy performances, and the Victorian Christmas Fayre, which takes place in the city centre in December.

# 21

The University of Worcester is a modern university with a strong reputation for teaching and research.

The university is home to around 10,000 students and offers a wide range of courses, including nursing, teacher training and sports science.

# 22

Worcester is known for its beautiful parks and green spaces, including Gheluvelt Park and Cripplegate Park.

These parks offer a range of activities, from children's play areas to sports facilities and picnic areas.

# 23

Worcester is home to a number of museums and galleries, including the Worcester City Art Gallery and Museum, which houses a collection of local art and historical artefacts.

Other notable museums include the Royal Worcester Porcelain Museum and the George Marshall Medical Museum.

# 24

Worcester's historic Guildhall is a Grade I listed building that dates back to the 18th century. The building has been used for a variety of purposes over the years, including as a courthouse, a meeting hall and a theatre.

# 25

Everyone loves Christmas! The Worcester Victorian Christmas Fayre is an annual event that takes place in the city centre in December.

The fayre features over 200 stalls selling festive gifts, crafts and food, as well as a range of entertainment and activities.

# 26

Worcester is known for its traditional pubs, many of which have been serving ale for centuries. The city is home to a number of historic pubs, including the Cardinal's Hat, which dates back to the 14th century.

# 27

The Worcester Festival of Light is an annual event that takes place in the city centre in November. The festival features a range of light installations, performances and activities, and attracts visitors from across the region.

# 28

The Hive is a state-of-the-art library and information centre in Worcester that is shared by the University of Worcester and the city council.

The building features a striking honeycomb-like design and is a popular spot for studying and research.

# 29

Worcester is a popular destination for foodies, with a range of restaurants and cafes offering local and international cuisine. The city is particularly well-known for its seafood, with fresh catches from the nearby coast served in many of its restaurants.

# 30

Worcester is well-connected to the rest of the UK, with excellent road and rail links to major cities such as Birmingham and London.

The city is also easily accessible by air, with Birmingham International Airport just a short drive away.

# 31

The Worcester Bosch Group is a leading manufacturer of heating and hot water products, and is headquartered in Worcester. The company has a long history in the city, dating back to the early 1960s, and is one of the city's largest employers.

# 32

Worcester has a thriving theatre scene, with a range of venues throughout the city, including the Swan Theatre and the Huntingdon Hall.

The city is also home to the Worcester Repertory Company, which produces a range of plays and performances

# 33

The Worcester Music Festival is an annual event that takes place in the city every September.

The festival features a range of musical performances, from jazz and blues to rock and pop, and is free to attend.

# 34

As Worcester has been growing since Roman times, there are mnay historic and ancient buildings, most of which are still in use, including the Worcester Cathedral, which dates back to the 7th century, and the Greyfriars' House and Garden, which dates back to the 15th century.

# 35

The Worcester Exhibition was an art exhibit inspired by the Great London Exhibition. In 1882 the city hosted sections for fine art, sculpture and historical documents.

It was a great success and profits raised helped build the Victoria Institute which today is the city art gallery and museum.

# 36

The Worcester Woods Country Park is a large park on the outskirts of the city, featuring over 100 acres of woodland, meadows, and lakes.

The park is popular with families, hikers, and nature lovers.

# 37

The Worcester St John's Cycling Club is one of the oldest cycling clubs in the UK, and was founded in 1885. The club offers a range of events and activities for cyclists of all levels, including training sessions and social rides.

# 38

The Worcester City Art Gallery and Museum is one of the city's most popular cultural attractions, and features a collection of over 300,000 artefacts, including local art, pottery, and natural history exhibits.

# 39

The Worcester Racecourse is a popular destination for horse racing enthusiasts, and hosts a range of events and races throughout the year. The racecourse also offers a range of facilities for visitors, from restaurants and bars to conference rooms and wedding venues.

# 40

Worcester is a popular destination for walkers and hikers, with a range of trails and routes throughout the city and its surrounding countryside. The Worcester Way and the Worcestershire Way are two popular long-distance walking routes in the area.

# 41

The Worcester Show is an annual event that takes place in the city every August. The show features a range of competitions and displays, from gardening and baking to arts and crafts, and is free to attend.

# 42

The Worcester City Run is an annual event that takes place in the city every September. The run features a range of distances and challenges, from a half marathon to a fun run, and attracts runners from across the region.

# 43

The city was also an important centre for the glove-making industry during the 18th and 19th centuries, and many fine examples of Worcester gloves can be found in local museums and collections.

It peaked at the end of the 18th century when over half the glove making population of England were based in Worcester.

# 44

Swans are an iconic feature of Worcester, and are often seen swimming on the River Severn and its tributaries. The swans are a protected species in the UK, and are looked after by the city's Swan Sanctuary, which is run by volunteers.

# 45

Every year, the city holds a Swan Upping ceremony, which involves counting and tagging the swans to ensure their protection. The ceremony dates back to medieval times, and is now an important tradition in Worcester's calendar. The swans are also a popular tourist attraction, and visitors can often be seen feeding and photographing them along the river banks.

# 46

The Worcester Cathedral dominates the skyline of the city and is a tourist attraction, with people coming from miles around.

It is dedicated to St Mary and was originally built as a monastery by Bishop Bosel in 680 AD.

# 47

There's even a King buried in the cathedral.

King John reigned up until 1216 and instead of being buried in London as was the tradition, he was lain to rest in Worcester.

It was his choice to be buried there as he loved the area so much. He can be found in a place of honour in front of the High Alter.

# 48

The British Medical Association or BMA was founded in what is now Worcester University.

In 1832 it was the Royal Worcester Infirmary and it was here, in the board room, that it was founded.

# 49

John and Henry invented one of the best sauces ever. I'm talking about John Wheeley Lea and William Henry Perrins, AKA Lea & Perrins!

These two pharmacists created Worcestershire Sauce and is now known the world over and of course it was invented in Worcester!

# 50

There are four places twinned with Worcester.

Close to home, in France, is Vesinet, and a little further afield in Germany is Kleve. Ukmerge in Lithuania is the newest location to be twinned.

Over the other side of the Atlantic, in Massachusetts, USA, is the furthest place, also called Worcester!

# 51

You associate Shakespeare with Stratford-Upon-Avon, but Stratford was part of Worcestershire in Shakespeares day.

It is thought thought that he married Anne Hathaway in St Martins church in Worcester.

# 52

The Tudor House Museum is located in the oldest street in the city, and inside features the only original embossed ceiling in Worcester!

# 53

There have been several famous faces call Worcester their home.

What if I was to say the King in the North called it home from the age of 11? Know who I mean?

Game of Thrones star Kit Harrington grew up in the city and fondly remembers it.

## 54

It can also be a real hinderence to be located on the River Severn. it is always flooding!

The highest flood was recorded way back in 1795, but it does flood almost yearly.

The cricket ground is known for flooding roughly every 3 years or so. In the year 2000 there was a flood notes as one of the worst in 100 years, with the river rising 5 meters more than usual, destroying homes.

# 55

The rolling green hills of Malvern are said to have inspired the classic Narnia series by C S Lewis.

Still today there are dozens of working oil lamps in the area, and when it snows it looks exactly like the area written about in the childrens books. C S Lewis often walked the area and even met fellow fantasy writer J R R Tolkien in the Unicorn Pub.

# 56

The oldest newspaper in the entire UK is said to be the Berrow' Worcester Journal.

It was first published regularly in 1709 but started life in 1690 under the name the Worcester Postman.

# 57

Worcester is trying to start a new tradition. The Worcester Balloon Festival!

Hot Air Balloons will fill the sky, taking off from Worcester Racecourse.

There was a slight hitch in the plan to start, as the original dates in May had to be postponed due to stormy weather!

# 58

The White Witch of Worcester was a real person! Her name was Ursula Corbett and she was actually burned at the stake for poisoning her husband of only 3 weeks.

The stake itself is thought to have been places right in front of the Guildhall.

Witches are real!

# 59

If the supernatural is your thing then head north a few miles out of Worcester to the tiny hamlet of Claines, to The Mug House pub, as it's one of only two in the country that's actually built on consecrated ground!

News of bangs, smashes and paranormal sights have been reported and it's known as the most haunted pub in Worcestershire.

# 60

Worcester has a huge employment in engineering, a whopping 85% more than the national average!

Specifically machine engineering employment, since 2017, has been seen as a great success story in Worcester.

# 61

The final battle of the English Civil War happened in Worcester, and yes we've mentioned that previously, but the war started and ended in Worcestershire.

The war started in Powick Bridge, just south of Worcester in 1642, and ended in Worcester itself 9 years later in 1651.

# 62

Corporal punishment came to
and end in Worcester in 1862,
when local man William Ockold
was hanged.

He was arrested for the beating
and murder of his wife whilst
inebriated, and paid the
ultimate price.

# 63

The world renounced Royal Worcester Pottery heralds from the city.

The creators of fine pottery, figurines and more is also over 250 years old! It was founded in the year 1751 and is still going, and growing strong today!

# 64

The humble Morris minor car came from the brain of Worcester man William Morris.

William Richard Morris was also the 1st viscount Nuffield. He founded Morris Minor and also the Nuffield Foundation, which today includes the national Nuffield Health gyms.

A true entreprenuer!

# 65

The city used to have much more medievil architecture than it currently does, even as recent as the 1960's.

The city decided to demolish, then rebuild on the land. It was described as an act of self mutilation. Thankfully there is still many medieval locations around the city that survive today.

# 66

Worcester once had a castle!

It was built in the year 1068 on behalf of William the Conqueror. It was used extensively in the 12th and 13th century in the war against King John entitled the Barons War.

A jail was built at the castle but the rets went unused for some time. After a short while it became redundant and now nothing remains of the castle.

# 67

As well as football, the city is the home of the Worcester Wolves, a basketball team. Up until recently they plied their trade in the top tier of English basketball, but they now find themselves a few rungs down the ladder.

They were founded in the year 2000.

# 68

In the centre of Worcester you cannot miss the huge spire of what was the Church of St Andrew. This spire is now left all alone and is known as Glover's Needle.

At night the spire glows blue as a symbol representing St Andrew of Scotland.

# 69

As you walk along the path that leads to the cathedral next to the River Severn, you'll find brass plaques.

These plaques represent where the high waterlinemrose to in the flood of 1670 and subsequent floodings.

# 70

The picturesque bridge that crosses the River Severn was originally the only bridge in the South Midlands. It has been located in the same place since the 14th century but has been upgraded throughout time.

It was widened in 1931 to cope with the increase in traffic.

# 71

The Commandery is where the Royalists called their headquarters in the final war of the English Civil War also known as the Battle of Worcester.

You can visit it today as it's been transformed into a museum complete with delicious tea shop!

# 72

The oldest pub in Worcester is The Cardinal's Hat, and can be dated back to the year 1497!

Over the years it has had many names including The Swan and Falcon and the Coventry Arms. The pub is only 2 rooms big but head down into the cellar and the history gets older, as it could be dated back to the 1300s!

And of course, it's haunted by a young girl ghost.

# 73

Another pub that's historically important is the King Charles house. Built in 1577, this was the hideout for King Charles at the battle of Worcester.

He hid away here and managed to escape in 1657. It was first used as a pub, but has seen many businesses pass through it. Recently in 2022 is was returned to a pub and restaurant and now serves award winning food!

# 74

The railway finally reached Worcester in 1850, although the only train running ran through to Birmingham and that was it. More were added and in 1863 the Great Western Railway was added to the Worcester station.

# 75

If the Germans would have invaded England during WWII then Worcester was the chosen city of to seat the government, keeping them away from London.

Thankfully this never occurred and the 16000 plus safely stayed in the capital, along with Winston Churchill.

# 76

The coat of Arms for Worcester is unique, in that it is essentially 2 together. The ancient arms depicts the castle, now no longer in existance, whilst the modern arms includes three pears.

Although it is called the 'modern' arms, it dates back to 1634 and speaks of a visit from Queen Elizabeth I in 1575, who possibly saw a pear tree and asked for three pears to be added the the coat of arms.

# 77

Queen Elizabeth I visited the city on August 13th 1575 and the city folk were asked to whitewash their house, or white-lime and colour it.

The Dean of the Cathedral presented the Queen with a gift of £20, about a years salary!

# 78

If you're of as certain age you'll probably remember the Kays catalogue. This was founded in Worcester way back in 1880!

Over the years the location moved around the city but it was always based there. That is until 2008 when the most recent warehouse was demolished.

# 79

Elgar is celebrated so much in the city that in 1981 a statue was unveiled of the composer, designed by Kenneth Potts.

It is located just a few yards away from where his dad used to run his music shop on Worcester High Street.

# 80

Every August Worcester plays host to the biggest CAMRA beer festival in the West Midlands, and one of the biggets ten in the whoe of the UK.

Over 14000 people attend this annual event to taste creations from across the city and beyond.

**81**

A recent annual event in Worcester is the Vegan Market which started in 2021.

It is due to continue to take place twice a year in spring and in Autumn, and dozens of vegan stalls will fill Worcester High Street and the Cathedral Square.

# 82

One of the 18th centuries most well regarded actresses of tragedy first took to the floorboards of the Theatre Royal.

Sarah Siddons was born in Wales and went on to be one of Englands most well respected and well known actresses.

# 83

In 1241 Worcester hosted a gathering of the most well respected Jews in the country. The Bishopric didn't take too kindly to the gathering and Jews and pushed against them for segregation.

In 1275 after years of violence they left the city and moved to the nearby Hereford.

# 84

If you're not local to Worcester you may not be too sure on how to pronounce it.

Worsester?
Werkester?
Wooster?

Nope. The way the city is pronounced by the locals is Wuss-ter.

# 85

Worcester makes several appearances in the film series Shrek.
Director of the third film, Chris Miller, went as far as to say that they even wrote songs about it but had to cut out.

He revealed that the name is so hard to pronounce yet people love the sauce in the states, and so the jokes kept flowing!

# 86

Although the city is twinneed with 4 other locations across the globe, many more places have taken the name Worcester.

South Africa has Worcester Southern Cape, Zambia has Worcester Limpopo, Jamaica has Worcester - Saint Catherine and even the Worcester Summit in the Pensacola, Antarctica!

# 87

Worcester Cathedral is magnificent in so many ways, and it also boast a world first.

The 12th Century Chapter house is thought to be the very first in the world to be designed circular.

# 88

The Worcester and Birmingham canal celebrated it's 200th year in 2015.

The celebrations lasted for 3 days and took in local musicians, artists and makers in a large scale festival..

# 89

Between 1771 and 2002 the Worcester Royal Infirmary operated.
In 1932 it was given the Royal status as HRH Prince of Wales visited.

Since 2002 it has become an interactive museum.

# 90

There have been world superstars perform in Worcester, albeit at the start of their career. The most notable is Ed Sheeran, where he performed at The Marrs Bar.

Also at the same venue acts such as Ellie Goulding, Bowling For Soup and Paul Young have performed. A true musical gem in the heart of Worcester.

# 91

Here's one for the record books, literally!

The longest living rabbit came from Worcester, and I mean long as in length!

Darius was a Flemish giant rabbit and was measured as being 4 foot and 3 inches long, claiming the record on April 6th 2010!

# 92

Another record to note is held by BBC Hereford and Worcester. It's one of the most bizarre records too.

in 2011 they claimed the record for the most people dressed as garden gnomes! 478 people donned their stripy tights and green and red hats to help raise money for Children in Need.

# 93

Future US presidents John Adams and Thomas Jefferson visited Worcester.

In 1786 they visited Fort Royal Hill, the location of the final battle in the civil war.

# 94

Prior to the civil war, the spaces between the streets of Worcester were filled witrh greens and even orchards.

Once the civil war ended, the city's  population grew and so expansion was needed, so these were lost to new houses.

# 95

There are now three railway station sin Worcester.
Up until recently Worcester Foregate Street and Worcester Shrub Hill were the only ones in operation, but in 2020 the Worcester Parkway opened.

# 96

Diglis Bridge is the newest bridge to be built to cross the River Severn.

It opened in 2010 on July 20th and is a dedicated cycle and pedestrian bridge.
It is one of only 2 bridges in the whole world that the cable-stayed tower incline is towards the river span.

# 97

Comedians from across the UK have visited Worcester to perform to packed out audiences.

The Huntingdon Hall has seen the likes of Eddie Izzard, Jack Dee and Jason Manford perform.

# 98

As well as the Royal Infirmary museum, there is also a museum looking at 250 years of medicine called the George Marshall museum.
George Marshall was a GP and former surgeon. The museum looks at the way medicine and health care has evolved and is a popular tourist attraction.

# 99

With Worcester located on the Rivr Severn, it only makes sense that there's a boat race!

Race The Dragon has been taking place for over 25 years and involves up to 30 teams including men, women, mixed and under 18 teams.

# 100

in the 16th century in Worcester, by law all men had to practice archery every Sunday afternoon!

This practice happened every Sunday afternoon at the area called The Butts.

# Your Own Facts!

_____

_____

_____

_____

_____

_____

_____

_____

_____

_____

_____

_____

# Your Own Facts!

_____

_____

_____

_____

_____

_____

_____

_____

_____

_____

_____

_____

# Your Own Facts!

_____

_____

_____

_____

_____

_____

_____

_____

_____

_____

_____

# Your Own Facts!

_____

_____

_____

_____

_____

_____

_____

_____

_____

_____

_____

_____

# Your Own Facts!

_____

_____

_____

_____

_____

_____

_____

_____

_____

_____

_____

Thanks for reading.

If you've enjoyed this book,
please leave me a
review on Amazon

*Lizzie Winters*

Printed in Dunstable, United Kingdom